CW00408984

Tony Bennett Autobiography

Sir Melody Burrows

Contents

Early Life And Childhood

Tony Bennett Was Born On August 3, 1926, In Astoria, Queens, New York City. He Is One Of The Most Well-Known And Adored Vocalists In The Annals Of American Music. Anthony Dominick Benedetto Was The Youngest Of The Three Children Born To Italian Immigrants John Benedetto And Anna Suraci Benedetto. His Birth Name Was Anthony Dominick Benedetto. Growing Up In A Working-Class Household During The Great Depression Had A Significant Impact On Bennett's Temperament, Work Ethic, And Musical Sensibility.

The Benedetto Family Had Financial Difficulties During The 1930s Great Depression. John, Tony's Father, Was A Grocery Store Employee, And Anna, His Mother, Was A Seamstress. Despite The Difficulties, The Love Of Music And The Arts In The Family Served As A Basis For Young Tony's Future Endeavors. Tony Was First

Exposed To Music By His Amateur Singer Father, Who Instilled In Him A Love Of The Sounds Of The Italian Operatic Tenors And The Era's Most Popular Songs.

Tony Bennett Showed Early On That He Had A Natural Ability For Singing And Performing. He Often Sang In Front Of His Loved Ones And Friends, Getting Compliments And Support For His Singing. Tony Had His Official Education At Public School 141 In Astoria, Where He Equally Loved Music And Sketching And Painting. Later, His Musical Career And Second Profession As A Painter Would Both Serve As Outlets For His Creative Abilities.

When Tony Was Barely 13 Years Old, His Family Experienced A Significant Change. Young Tony And His Siblings Were Left To Help Maintain The Family When Their Father Passed Away. Tony Started Doing A Variety Of Jobs, Such As Grocery Delivery

And Performing At Local Venues For Pitiful Compensation. He Learned The Importance Of Perseverance And Hard Effort From These Events, Which Would Be Useful Lessons For His Future Profession.

Despite His Difficulties, Tony's Love For Music Never Faded. When And When He Could, He Kept On Performing. Tony Bennett, At 17 Years Old, Took First Place In A Singing Competition On The Well-Known Radio Program "Arthur Godfrey's Talent Scouts" In 1943. His Life Was Changed By This Triumph Since It Gave Him The Chance To Play With Legendary Bandleader Bob Crosby.

Tony's Ground-Breaking Performance Led To Commitments In Several Nightclubs And Theaters Around The Nation. After Using The Stage Name "Joe Bari" For A While, He Eventually Switched To "Tony Bennett" On The Recommendation Of His First Agency,

Who Believed That The Name Change Would Appeal To A Wider Audience.

Tony Was Recognized By Renowned Singer And Actress Pearl Bailey In 1950 While Singing At A Bar In Greenwich Village. Bailey Asked Him To Perform As Her Opening Act At The Village Inn, A Famous Jazz Venue. Tony Bennett's Career Took A Big Stride Forward Because To This Engagement, Which Made Him Popular With Both Critics And Audiences.

At Around The Same Time, Bob Hope Learned About Tony's Skill And Invited Him To Travel With His Group. Tony Was Given The Chance To Play In Front Of A Larger Audience, And It Also Improved His Stage Presence And Performing Abilities. His Connection To Bob Hope Enhanced His Standing As A Budding Star In The Entertainment World.

Tony Bennett Secured A Contract With Columbia Records In 1951, And The Record Company Would Go On To Become His Longtime Home. His First Song, "Because Of You," Which Was Published In 1951, Shot To The Top Of The Charts And Became His First Gold Record. Tony Bennett Rose To Fame As A Result Of This Accomplishment And Was One Of The Top Pop Singers Of The 1950s.

Tony Bennett's Fame Soared Throughout The Decade With Success After Hit, Such As "Rags To Riches" And "Stranger In Paradise" (1953). His Distinct Vocal Delivery, Which Was Distinguished By A Warm, Expressive Voice And Perfect Phrasing, Struck A Chord With Listeners And Helped Him Develop A Devoted Following.

Tony Bennett's Successful Record Career Began With The Publication Of His First Lp, "Cloud 7," In 1954. His Records Demonstrated His Ability In Addressing Jazz

Standards And Show Tunes In Addition To His Skill At Performing Popular Songs. His Variety Distinguished Him From Many Other Modern Pop Artists And Won Him A Larger Fanbase.

The Song "I Left My Heart In San Francisco," Which Would Later Become Tony Bennett's Anthem And A Timeless Classic, Earned Him His First Grammy Award For "Best Solo Vocal Performance, Male" In 1956. Even Today, Tony Bennett's Name Is Inextricably Associated To The Song Because Of Its Legendary Position.

Tony Bennett's Fame Had Difficulties When The 1960s Got Underway Because Of The Emergence Of Rock & Roll And The British Invasion. Nevertheless, He Kept Developing And Modifying His Musical Approach, Playing With Other Genres And Working With Modern Musicians Like Count Basie, Duke Ellington, And Stan Getz. Tony's

Commitment To His Art And His Ongoing
Attraction To Devoted Followers Allowed
Him Maintain His Career Despite The
Shifting Musical Scene.

Tony Bennett Saw A Rebirth In Popularity In
The 1970s, In Part Due To The Critical
Success Of His Critically Acclaimed Record
"Tony Bennett At Carnegie Hall" (1962). He
Further Won Over Viewers By Hosting "The
Tony Bennett Show," A Popular Television
Variety Program.

Tony Bennett's Musical Career Continued To
Develop During The Next Decades. He
Collaborated On Duets With A Variety Of
Performers, Including Amy Winehouse,
Frank Sinatra, Paul Mccartney, Lady Gaga,
And Lady Gaga, Showcasing His Ability To
Work With Musicians Of Many Genres And
Ages.

Tony Bennett Has An Interest For Painting And Other Forms Of Art In Addition To His Singing Profession. He Started Painting In The Late 1970s, And Now He Is A Skilled Visual Artist. His Works Have Been Shown In Renowned Galleries And Museums Across The Globe, Contributing To His Creative Legacy In Yet Another Way.

Tony Bennett's Cd "Duets: An American Classic," Which Included Duets With Other Modern Musicians, Was Published In 2006. Tony Bennett's Place As A Legendary Figure In American Music Was Further Confirmed With This Album, Which Earned Several Grammy Awards.

Tony Bennett Has Received Countless Awards And Distinctions For His Services To Music, Both As A Musician And As The Guardian Of The Great American Songbook. He Has 20 Grammy Awards Under His Belt, Including A Lifetime Achievement Award

And Many Wins For Best Traditional Pop Vocal Album. He Received The Renowned Kennedy Center Honors In 2005 In Recognition Of His Lifetime Of Creative Accomplishment.

Tony Bennett Has Performed And Toured Successfully Into His Latter Years Despite His Advanced Age. He Is Admired By Artists And Spectators Alike For His Commitment To His Profession And His Capacity For Moving Performances.

In Addition To His Musical Abilities, Tony Bennett Is Renowned For His Charitable Work. He Has Relentlessly Fought To Promote Arts Programs In Schools And Has Been An Enthusiastic Advocate Of Arts Education. Tony Has Also Been A Steadfast Supporter Of Research Into Alzheimer's Disease, Promoting The Cause And Donating Money For It.

Tony Bennett's Life And Career, As Of My Most Recent Information Update In September 2021, Have Been Full With Triumphs, Setbacks, And Achievements. He Became A Worldwide Music Superstar After Beginning As A Little Child Singing For His Family, Demonstrating The Strength Of Talent, Effort, And Tenacity.

Beyond His Record-Breaking Sales And Critical Praise, Tony Bennett's Musical Legacy Had A Significant Effect On A Wide Range Of Genres. He Has Made An Enduring Contribution To American Music, Influencing Generations Of Musicians And Enhancing The Lives Of Countless Admirers All Around The Globe. The Events Of Tony Bennett's Youth And Upbringing Molded Him Into A Modest Person.

Birth And Family Background

The Legendary American Singer Tony Bennett Was Born Anthony Dominick Benedetto On August 3, 1926 In Astoria, Queens, New York City. His Parents, Italian Immigrants John Benedetto And Anna Suraci Benedetto, Came To America In The Early 20th Century In Pursuit Of Greater Prospects And A Brighter Future. The Circumstances Of Tony's Birth And Upbringing Provide An Intriguing Window Into The Cultural Influences That Formed His Life And Career.

Small-Town Podàrgoni, In The Southern Italian Province Of Calabria, Was The Hometown Of John Benedetto. He Came From A Hard-Working, Close-Knit Family And Was Born In 1895. When He Was Just 11 Years Old, John Immigrated To America In Pursuit Of Economic Prospects. He Looked For The Promise Of A Better Life In The "Land Of Opportunity," Like Many Other

Italian Immigrants Of His Period. After Relocating To New York City, John Got Employment As A Tailor, Helping The City's Expanding Apparel Sector.

Tony Bennett's Mother, Anna Suraci, Was Also Born There In 1897. She Was Raised In A Typical Italian Home Where Strong Family Connections And Cultural Values Were Valued Highly. Like Her Future Husband John, Anna Immigrated To America In 1908, When She Was Just 11 Years Old, In Hopes Of A Better Life. In Order To Establish Themselves In The New World, Her Family Relocated To The Bronx.

John And Anna Met In New York City In 1921 And Fell In Love. Because Of Their Common Italian Ancestry And Similar Immigration Experiences, They Had A Particularly Close Relationship. They Were Married In 1924, And Their Youngest Child, Anthony Dominick

Benedetto, Who Would Eventually Become Famous Across The Globe As Tony Bennett, Was Born Two Years Later.

Tony Was Born In America At A Period When Both Social And Economic Revolution Was Taking Place. The Jazz Age, Fast Industrialisation, And Urbanization All Took Place Throughout The 1920s. With The Harlem Revival Thriving In New York City And African American Authors And Artists Making Substantial Contributions To The Arts And Culture, It Was A Time Of Cultural Revival.

Tony Was Raised In A Small Apartment On 29th Street In Astoria, Queens, As A Young Kid. The Area Was A Cultural Melting Pot, Emulating The Bigger Immigrant Populations That Had Established In New York City. Tony Was Exposed To A Varied Tapestry Of Languages, Customs, And Foods At A Young Age, Which Helped Him Develop An

Appreciation For Cultural Diversity—A Topic That Would Later Resound In His Music And Way Of Life.

Children Of John And Anna Benedetto Were Raised With A Strong Sense Of Family Values. They Stressed The Value Of Patience, Hard Effort, And Thankfulness For The Possibilities They Had In America. The Benedetto Family Remained Close-Knit And Supportive Of One Another Despite Going Through Financial Difficulties Throughout The Great Depression.

Tony's Father Was A Key Figure In Encouraging His Passion Of Music Throughout His Childhood Years. The Family Enjoyed Listening To John Benedetto, An Amateur Singer, Perform Classic Italian Tunes. Tony's Early Exposure To His Father's Singing Had A Profound Impact On Him And Started His Interest In Music.

When Tony Was Just Ten Years Old, His Father Tragically Lost His Life When He Died Away Suddenly. Tony's Father's Passing Was A Pivotal Moment In His Life Since It Not Only Created A Gap In The Family But Also Made Young Tony Face The Harsh Facts Of Life And The Burden Of Providing For The Family.

Tony And His Siblings, John Jr. And Mary, Were Put In A Difficult Position When Their Father Passed Away. As The Family's Financial Position Deteriorated Further, Tony Was Forced To Assume Duties Beyond His Years. He Began Taking Odd Jobs, Such As Carrying Groceries And Singing In Small Venues For Pitiful Pay, To Help Support His Mother And Siblings.

Throughout This Trying Time, Tony's Love Of Music Gave Comfort And Served As A Vehicle For Emotional Expression. He Turned To Singing For Solace, And His

Musical Skill Grew. Despite The Challenges He Encountered, Tony Persevered In His Academic Work At Public School 141 In Astoria, Where He Also Shown A Strong Interest In Painting And Sketching.

Due To His Early Exposure To Music And Natural Aptitude, Tony Bennett Caught The Attention Of His Instructors And Classmates. Tony Yearned To Pursue A Singing And Performing Career Because Of Their Encouragement And The Music Of Performers Like Bing Crosby And Nat King Cole.

The Globe Was Still Struggling To Recover From The Terrible Effects Of The Great Depression When Tony Bennett Approached His Adolescence. With The Start Of World War Ii, The 1940s Saw The Emergence Of New Difficulties. The Family's Feeling Of Duty And Patriotism Was Increased At This

Period By The Military Service Of Tony's
Siblings, John Jr. And Mary.

Tony Joined The American Army In 1943, At
17 Years Old, As World War Ii Was Coming
To An End. His Love Of Music, Nevertheless,
Was Unaffected By His Service In The
Military. Tony Continued To Improve His
Singing Abilities And Delight His Fellow
Troops While Serving By Playing In A Military
Band.

Tony Returned To New York City After The
War With A Newfound Commitment To
Achieving His Musical Goals. He Furthered
His Performing Abilities And Voice Methods
By Enrolling At The American Theatre Wing
Professional School Via The G.I. Bill.

Tony's Big Break In The Music Business
Occurred In 1949 When He Won First Place
In A Singing Contest On The Well-Known
Radio Program "Arthur Godfrey's Talent

Scouts." He Was Given The Chance To Play With Legendary Bandleader Bob Crosby As A Result Of His Success. Around This Time, He Also Switched His Stage Name From "Joe Bari" To "Tony Bennett," Which Was Recommended By Bob Hope's Publicist Because He Thought It Would Be More Memorable And Appealing To A Wider Audience.

Tony Bennett Began His Successful Recording Career By Signing A Deal With Columbia Records At The Beginning Of The 1950s. His First Song, "Because Of You," Which Was Published In 1951, Shot To The Top Of The Charts And Became His First Gold Record. This Accomplishment Launched Tony Bennett Into Celebrity And Signaled The Start Of A Fruitful Musical Career That Would Last For Decades.

As Tony Bennett's Career Took Off, He Never Lost Sight Of The Principles His Immigrant

Parents Instilled In Him: Humility, Perseverance, And A Great Love For His Italian Ancestry. He Paid Tribute To His Background By Including Italian Songs In His Repertoire. He Also Often Sung In Italian While Performing, Which Helped Him To Connect With His Past And Broaden His Audience.

Tony Bennett Has Credited His Parents With Forming His Character And Work Ethic Throughout His Life. He Was Extremely Moved By Their Sacrifices And Challenges As Italian Immigrants Adjusting To Life In A New Nation, Which Motivated Him To Work As An Ambassador For Peace And Cultural Understanding.

Finally, Tony Bennett's Family And Place Of Birth Provide A Complex Tapestry Of Events That Had A Significant Impact On His Life And Work. Tony Was Raised In A Close-Knit Italian-American Family In New York City,

Where He Learned The Importance Of
Perseverance, Hard Work, And A Profound
Respect For Music And The Arts. Tony's
Interest For Music And The Arts Was
Cultivated By His Mother's Devotion To
Their Family And His Father's Love Of
Singing.

First Steps Into The Music Industry

Tony Bennett's Entry Into The Music Business Was Defined By Tenacity, Skill, And A String Of Crucial Events That Would Go On To Mold His Destiny As One Of The Most Recognizable Vocalists In The Annals Of American Music. Tony's Rise To Fame Was A Monument To His Love Of Music, Tenacity, And Unrelenting Dedication To His Profession, From His Early Performances In Local Settings To His Breakthrough On National Radio.

Tony Dominick Benedetto Was Raised In A Working-Class Italian Immigrant Household In Astoria, Queens, New York City. Tony Was Born Anthony Dominick Benedetto On August 3, 1926. His Parents, John Benedetto And Anna Suraci Benedetto, Prepared Him For His Future Endeavors In The Entertainment World By Instilling In Him A Strong Work Ethic And A Love Of Music.

Tony Bennett Had A Natural Ability For Singing From An Early Age. He Started Singing For Family And Friends After Being Inspired By The Time's Top Artists And His Father's Passion For Music. Tony Yearned To Become A Professional Singer, Inspired By Their Praise And Driven By His Love Of Music.

When Tony Was Barely 13 Years Old, Tragedy Hit The Family When His Father, John Benedetto, Passed Away Suddenly. Tony's Life Had A Major Turning Point With The Death Of His Father Since It Not Only Created A Gap In The Family But Also Put Financial Responsibility On His Young Shoulders.

Tony And His Siblings, John Jr. And Mary, Suffered Financial Difficulties When Their Father Passed Away, And He Was Forced To Work Many Jobs To Support The Family.

Despite The Difficulties, Tony's Passion For Music Persisted, And He Kept Playing Whenever And Whenever He Could.

Tony Bennett's Life Changed Dramatically In 1943 When, At The Age Of 17, He Enrolled In The U.S. Army During The Closing Stages Of World War Ii. Although His Time In The Military Interfered With His Attempts To Pursue A Career In Music, It Did Not Lessen His Love Of Singing. Tony Sang For His Fellow Troops And Continued To Hone His Performing Abilities While Serving In A Military Band.

Tony Returned To New York City After The War With A Newfound Commitment To Achieving His Musical Goals. He Used The G.I. Bill To Enrol In The American Theatre Wing's Professional School, Where He Sharpened His Skills And Sought To Improve His Vocal Range And Stage Presence.

During This Period, Tony Bennett's Ability Attracted The Notice Of The Appropriate Individuals, Opening The Door To A String Of Fortunate Meetings And Circumstances That Would Catapult Him Into The Limelight Of The Music Business.

Tony Bennett's Life Changed Significantly In 1949 When He Won A Singing Contest On The Well-Known Radio Program "Arthur Godfrey's Talent Scouts." The Fact That He Got To Play With Legendary Bandleader Bob Crosby Thanks To This Triumph Was A Turning Point In His Career.

Tony's Triumph On "Arthur Godfrey's Talent Scouts" Made Him Known To A Wider Audience And Caught The Attention Of Business Experts. Music Industry Professionals Were Drawn To His Silky Voice And Perfect Phrasing, Which Opened The Door For A Record Contract With A Big Label.

Around This Time, Tony Bennett Changed
His Stage Identity To "Joe Bari" In Order To
Sing In Nearby Venues And Further His
Musical Career. But Destiny Stepped In
When He Ran Into Bob Hope's Publicist,
Who Recommended That He Switch His
Stage Name To Something More Distinctive
And Attractive To A Wider Audience. At That
Point, He Acquired The Moniker "Tony
Bennett," Which Would Quickly Come To
Stand For A Particular, Alluring Singing Style.

Tony Bennett Secured A Recording Contract
With Columbia Records, One Of The Most
Esteemed Record Companies Of The Time,
In 1950. This Was An Important Milestone In
His Entry Into The Music Business Since It
Gave Him A Venue To Record And
Disseminate His Songs To A Larger Audience.

"Boulevard Of Broken Dreams," His First
Song With Columbia Records, Was Released

In 1950. Despite Not Being An Immediate Smash, The Song Launched Tony Bennett's Music Career And Laid The Groundwork For What Was To Come.

Despite The Lackluster Performance Of His First Song, Tony Bennett's Career Started To Take Off With Following Singles. He Made "Because Of You," A Song That Would Go On To Become His First Big Success And A Pivotal Moment In His Career, In 1951. Tony Received His First Gold Record When The Song Ascended The Charts And Peaked At Number One.

The Song "Because Of You" Demonstrated Tony Bennett's Vocal Skills And His Capacity To Express Emotion Through Song. His Warm, Expressive Voice Connected With Listeners, Making Him Stand Out As A Unique And Alluring Artist.

Tony Bennett's Ascent To Fame As A Result Of The Success Of "Because Of You" Saw Him Swiftly Establish Himself As One Of The Top Pop Performers Of The 1950s. He Further Cemented His Status As A Rising Star In The Music Business With His Later Recordings, Which Included "Cold, Cold Heart" (1951) And "Rags To Riches" (1953).

Tony Bennett's Fame Increased, Making Him A Sought-After Musician Who Attracted Sizable And Devoted Crowds To His Live Performances. Each Presentation Was An Unforgettable Experience Because To His Charisma, Charm, And Connection With The Crowd Throughout His Live Performances.

Midway Through The 1950s, Tony Bennett Broadened His Musical Catalog And Started Experimenting With Jazz Classics And Show Songs, Showcasing His Vocal Ability. He Stood Out From Many Other Current Singers Because To His Ability To Switch Between

Pop, Jazz, And Classic Pop Genres With Ease. This Endearing Quality Made Him Popular With A Variety Of Audiences.

Jazz Standards Were Included On Tony Bennett's 1956 Album "Tony," Which Was Made Available To The Public. His Career Took Off With The Release Of The Record, Which Revealed Him As A Multifaceted Musician Who Had A Strong Affinity For The Great American Songbook. Tony Bennett's Status As An Interpreter Of Timeless Music Officially Began With This, And It Would Last For Decades.

Tony Bennett's Career Remained Successful As The 1950s Drew To A Conclusion, And He Remained A Significant Player In The Music Business. However, The 1960s Would Bring Fresh Difficulties And Modifications To The Music Industry That Would Put His Resiliency And Capacity For Adaptation To The Test.

Many Classic Pop Performers, Notably Tony Bennett, Had Difficulties In The 1960s As Rock & Roll And The British Invasion Gained Popularity. Nevertheless, He Kept Developing And Changing His Musical Aesthetic While Maintaining His Creative Integrity.

Tony Bennett's Seminal Recording "Tony Bennett At Carnegie Hall," Which Featured Him Performing Live, Was Made Available To The Public In 1962. His Image As A Great Performer Was Further Cemented By The Record, Which Was Met With Critical Praise.

Tony Bennett Continued To Record And Release New Music Throughout The 1960s And 1970s, Experimenting With Various Genres And Working With Other Musicians. His Reputation As A Versatile And Well-Respected Performer In Both The Pop And Jazz Worlds Was Further Cemented When

He Collaborated On Records With Jazz
Greats Like Count Basie And Stan Getz.

Tony Bennett's Fame Lasted Despite The
Difficulties Brought On By Shifting Musical
Preferences, In Part Because Of His Devoted
Fan Base And His Capacity To Engage
Audiences Via His Moving Performances.

Tony Bennett's Reputation Grew Again In
The 1980s, In Part Due To A New Generation
Of Admirers Discovering His Work. His
Association With Modern Musicians Like
K.D. Lang And The Red Hot Chili Peppers
Helped Him Reach Younger Audiences And A
New Generation Of Music Fans.

"The Good Life: The Autobiography Of Tony
Bennett," Released In 1986, Is A Genuine
And Intimate Account Of Tony Bennett's Life
And Career. The Book Gave Readers A
Glimpse Into His Problems, Victories, And

Adventures, Further Endearing Him To His Readers.

The Cd "Mtv Unplugged: Tony Bennett," Which Included His Classic Songs With Performances By Modern Musicians, Was Released In The 1990s, Catapulting Tony Bennett's Career To New Heights. The Record Received Favorable Reviews And Introduced Tony Bennett To A Whole New Group Of Admirers.

Tony Bennett Maintained A Vigorous Recording And Touring Schedule Throughout The 2000s And 2010s, Displaying Amazing Endurance And An Unrelenting Dedication To His Art. His Duets With Diverse Musicians, Such As Lady Gaga, Amy Winehouse, And Andrea Bocelli, Increased His Popularity And Kept Enthralling Audiences All Over The Globe.

Tony Bennett Followed His Interest For Painting In Addition To His Great Singing Career. He Started Painting In The Late 1970s, And Now He Is A Skilled Visual Artist. His Artwork Has Been Shown At Renowned Galleries And Museums Throughout The Globe, Contributing To His Artistic Legacy In Yet Another Way.

Numerous Awards And Recognitions Have Been Given To Tony Bennett In Recognition Of His Services To The Music Business. He Has Won Best Traditional Pop Vocal Album Many Times And A Lifetime Achievement Award Among His 20 Grammy Awards. He Received The Coveted Kennedy Center Honors In 2005 To Recognize His Lifetime Of Creative Excellence.

Beyond His Work In Music And The Arts, Tony Bennett Has Been A Fierce Supporter Of Both Alzheimer's Disease Research And Arts Education. To Provide Aspiring Artists A

Top-Notch Arts Education, He Founded The
Frank Sinatra School Of The Arts In Queens,
New York.

Tony Bennett Revealed In 2021 That He Had
Been Given An Alzheimer's Disease
Diagnosis, An Illness That Impairs Memory
And Cognitive Abilities. He Continued To
Perform And Record Music In Spite Of This
Prognosis, Displaying His Talent And
Fortitude Both As A Musician And As A
Person.

To Sum Up, Tony Bennett's Entry Into The
Music Business Was Characterized By A
Blend Of Skill, Tenacity, And Fortunate
Circumstances That Helped Him Become
One Of The Most Renowned Vocalists In
American Music History. Tony's Rise To
Fame, Which Began With Early
Performances In Intimate Settings And
Culminated With His Breakthrough On
National Radio, Is A Testament To His

Unrelenting Dedication To His Craft, His Love Of Music, And His Capacity For Growth As An Artist. His Long Reputation As An Interpreter Of The Great American Songbook And His Ongoing Commitment To His Craft Have Won Him The Respect And Adoration Of Music Lovers Everywhere. For Many Years To Come, Tony Bennett's Contributions To The Music Business And His Influence As A Cultural Ambassador Will Be Honored.

Impact On Music And Popular Culture

The Influence Of Tony Bennett On Music And Popular Culture Is Profound And Extensive. Tony Bennett's Brilliance, Creativity, And Lasting Appeal Have Created An Enduring Impression On The Entertainment Industry, Making Him One Of The Most Admired And Adored Singers In American Music History. Tony Bennett's Legacy Is One Of Inspiration, Originality, And Enduring Relevance, From His Unique Vocal Style To His Contributions To The Great American Songbook, His Impact On Other Musicians, And His Position As A Cultural Ambassador.

The Great American Songbook And The Interpretation Of Classics: Tony Bennett's Musical Career Has Been Centered On His Profound Respect For The Great American Songbook, A Collection Of Timeless Songs From The Early To Mid-20th Century. He

Became Well-Known For His Superb Renditions Of Vintage Classics, Giving Them Fresh Life And Making Them Accessible To New Audiences. He Was Able To Capture The Soul Of Each Song And Make Them Distinctively His Own Thanks To His Ability To Communicate Passion, Perfect Phrasing, And Emotional Resonance.

Unique Vocal Style And Phrasing: Tony Bennett Is Readily Recognized Thanks To His Warm, Velvety Voice And Distinctive Vocal Style. He Stands Himself As A Master Singer Due To His Easy Switch Between Sweet Crooning And Thunderous Performances. He Has Won Praise From Journalists And Other Musicians Alike For His Deft Phrasing And Attention To Detail In Each Performance.

Cultural Ambassador: Tony Bennett Has Served As A Cultural Ambassador Throughout His Career, Supporting American Music And Art Both Domestically

And Abroad. He Has Traveled The World For His Concerts And Shows, Representing American Culture And Music With Style And Elegance. As An Ambassador, He Promoted Cross-Cultural Dialogue And Understanding While Showcasing The Finest Of American Creative Legacy.

Jazz And Traditional Pop Revival: Tony Bennett's Commitment To These Genres Helped Keep Them Alive And Current At A Time When Rock & Roll And Other Genres Were Gaining Popularity. He Continued To Draw Crowds With His Ageless Sound While Staying Faithful To His Musical Heritage And Adjusting To Shifting Preferences.

The Flexibility Of Tony Bennett As An Artist Is Shown By His Capacity To Reinvent Himself And Draw In New Audiences During The Course Of His Career. He Was Exposed To New Generations Via Collaborations With Modern Musicians Like Lady Gaga And The

Red Hot Chili Peppers, And His Ageless Appeal Connected With Followers Of All Ages.

Tony Bennett Has Left A Lasting Legacy In Music, And His Accomplishments Have Been Universally Praised. He Is One Of The Most Honored Performers In Grammy History With 20 Awards, Including A Lifetime Achievement Award. His Influence On The Music Business Goes Beyond Album Sales And Accolades; It Can Also Be Heard In The Work Of Innumerable Musicians Who Have Drawn Inspiration From Him.

Tony Bennett Has Had A Broad Impact On Current Artists Working In A Variety Of Disciplines. His Records With Musicians Like Lady Gaga, Amy Winehouse, And John Legend Have Received Critical Praise, And They Have Also Helped Him Reach New Audiences. Bennett Is A Source Of Inspiration For Young Singers Since So Many

Musicians Have Praised His Vocal Prowess, Phrasing, And Capacity For Audience Connection.

Iconic Song "I Left My Heart In San Francisco": One Of Tony Bennett's Most Famous Songs, "I Left My Heart In San Francisco," Has Come To Symbolize The City And Is Regarded As A Timeless Masterpiece Of American Music. The 1962 Song Is Now A Mainstay Of Bennett's Live Performances And Earned Him His Second Grammy Award For Record Of The Year.

Impact On Culture Of "I Left My Heart In San Francisco": Tony Bennett And The City It Honors Have Unique Meanings For "I Left My Heart In San Francisco." The Song Was Adopted As San Francisco's Unofficial Anthem And Is Played Often Across The City. Its Ongoing Appeal Has Cemented Its Position In The City's And The Country's Cultural Landscape.

Tony Bennett's Influence On The New York City Music Scene May Be Attributed To The Fact That He Was Born And Raised There And Has Always Loved The City. He Has Become A Beloved Character In The City's Music Scene Thanks To His Concerts And Appearances There, And He Continues To Be Strongly Linked To New York's Cultural History.

Tony Bennett As An Artistic Role Model: Tony Bennett Is An Artistic Role Model For Budding Artists Due To His Commitment To His Craft, Professionalism, And Longevity In The Music Business. Many Young Artists Have Been Motivated To Follow Their Aspirations And Professions With Enthusiasm And Dedication By His Ability To Remain Current And Preserve Creative Integrity.

"Duets: An American Classic" Has Significant Cultural Significance.

"Duets: An American Classic," A Seminal Cd By Tony Bennett, Was Released In 2006 And Included Cross-Genre Collaborations With Modern Musicians. The Album's Popularity Not Only Highlighted Bennett's Flexibility But Also The Great American Songbook's Lasting Appeal In Modern Music.

Contribution To Music Education: Tony Bennett Has Funded Programs To Encourage Music And The Arts In Schools As A Major Supporter Of Arts Education. He Has Fought To Make Sure That Music Education Is Available To Future Generations Because He Understands How Important It Is To Provide Kids The Chance To Develop Their Creative Abilities.

Art And The Visual Arts: In Addition To His Musical Career, Tony Bennett's Love Of Painting And Other Visual Arts Has Played A

Key Role In His Creative Development. His Paintings Have Been Shown In Galleries And Museums All Over The Globe, And His Work Has Become Well Known In The Art World.

Tony Bennett's Success As A Painter Has Encouraged Other Artists To Experiment With New Kinds Of Artistic Expression. His Success In Both Music And The Visual Arts Shows How Closely Related The Many Creative Mediums Are To One Another And Serves As A Reminder That Artistic Brilliance Knows No Bounds.

Work In Charity And Humanitarian Causes: Tony Bennett's Influence Goes Beyond Music And The Arts. He Has Been Actively Engaged In Charity Work, Supporting A Range Of Causes Such As Humanitarian Aid, Alzheimer's Disease Research, And Arts Education.

Tony Bennett And The Frank Sinatra School Of The Arts: In Astoria, Queens, New York City, Tony Bennett Established The Frank Sinatra School Of The Arts. The Goal Of The School Is To Provide Young Pupils Access To A Top-Notch Arts Education That Will Enable Them To Develop Their Artistic Abilities And Seek Jobs In The Field.

Tony Bennett's Influence On Film And Television: Over The Years, A Number Of Movies And Television Programs Have Included Tony Bennett's Music, Further Enhancing His Influence On Popular Culture. His Classic Tunes Have Been Used As The Music For Enduring Events And Moments In Television And Movies.

Tony Bennett's Influence On Commercialization And Advertising: Tony Bennett Is More Well-Known In Popular Culture As A Result Of His Songs Being Included In Commercials. His Music Has

Come To Be Associated With Class And Refinement, Making It An Obvious Option For Businesses Looking To Project A Classic Appeal.

Tony Bennett Has Earned Various Accolades And Awards Throughout The Course Of His Career In Acknowledgment Of His Contributions To Music And Popular Culture. These Include A Number Of Grammy Awards, Honorary Doctorates, And, Among Other Things, A Star On The Hollywood Walk Of Fame.

Tony Bennett's Music Continues To Resonate With Audiences Of All Ages: Tony Bennett's Live Concerts Continue To Draw Passionate Crowds Throughout The Globe. His Performances Have Evolved Into Occasions To Honor And Appreciate His Creative Legacy, Attracting Admirers Across Generations.

Performances On Television And Film

Tony Bennett's Performances On Television And Film Have Played A Significant Role In Showcasing His Talent, Expanding His Audience, And Solidifying His Status As One Of The Most Iconic Singers In American Music History. From His Early Appearances On Variety Shows To His Memorable Collaborations With Fellow Artists, Tony's Presence On Screen Has Left A Lasting Impact On Audiences Worldwide. This Exploration Of His Performances In Television And Film Will Delve Into The Memorable Moments That Have Contributed To His Enduring Popularity And Cultural Significance.

"Toast Of The Town" (Later Known As "The Ed Sullivan Show"):
Tony Bennett Made His First Television Appearance On "Toast Of The Town," Hosted By Ed Sullivan, In The Early 1950s.

His Performances On The Show Helped Introduce His Music To A National Audience And Played A Pivotal Role In Establishing His Career As A Rising Star In The Entertainment Industry. Sullivan's Show Was One Of The Most Popular Variety Programs Of Its Time, Providing An Invaluable Platform For Tony To Showcase His Vocal Talent And Captivating Stage Presence.

"The Perry Como Show":
In 1954, Tony Bennett Appeared On "The Perry Como Show," Another Popular Variety Program Of The Era. His Performances On The Show Allowed Him To Reach A Broader Audience And Further Solidify His Position As A Prominent Singer In The Music Industry. Como, A Fellow Italian-American Singer, And Host, Welcomed Tony As A Guest Performer On Multiple Occasions, Fostering A Sense Of Camaraderie Between The Two Artists.

"The Ed Sullivan Show":
Throughout The 1950s And 1960s, Tony
Bennett Was A Frequent Guest On "The Ed
Sullivan Show." His Performances On The
Show Featured A Diverse Selection Of Songs,
Showcasing His Ability To Interpret Various
Genres With Ease And Finesse. Sullivan's
Program Was A Platform For Top Talent,
And Tony's Appearances Solidified His Place
Among The Great Entertainers Of His Time.

"Tony Bennett: An American Classic" (2006):
In 2006, Nbc Aired A Television Special Titled
"Tony Bennett: An American Classic" In
Honor Of Tony's 80th Birthday. The Special,
Directed By Rob Marshall, Celebrated Tony's
Extraordinary Career And Featured
Appearances By Numerous Artists, Including
Christina Aguilera, John Legend, And Elton
John. The Show Combined Music
Performances, Interviews, And Vignettes
About Tony's Life, Offering Viewers A

Comprehensive Tribute To The Legendary Singer.

"Tony Bennett Celebrates 90: The Best Is Yet To Come" (2016):
In 2016, Nbc Broadcasted "Tony Bennett Celebrates 90: The Best Is Yet To Come," A Star-Studded Television Special Commemorating Tony Bennett's 90th Birthday. The Event Featured Performances By A Wide Array Of Artists, Including Lady Gaga, Stevie Wonder, And Andrea Bocelli, Paying Tribute To Tony's Musical Legacy. The Special Highlighted Tony's Impact On Music And Popular Culture, And It Became One Of The Most-Watched Television Events Of The Year.

"An All-Star Tribute To Tony Bennett" (2017):
In 2017, Pbs Aired "An All-Star Tribute To Tony Bennett," A Special Program Celebrating Tony's Remarkable Career. The

Show Featured Performances And Tributes By Esteemed Artists Such As Billy Joel, Lady Gaga, And Michael Bublé, Underscoring Tony's Lasting Influence On Contemporary Musicians And His Enduring Popularity.

Collaborations With Lady Gaga:
Tony Bennett's Collaborations With Lady Gaga Have Been Some Of The Most Notable Highlights Of His Television Performances. Their Chemistry On Stage And Their Unique Interpretations Of Classic Songs Have Garnered Widespread Acclaim. They First Collaborated On The Album "Cheek To Cheek" (2014), Which Featured Jazz Standards And Became A Commercial Success. Their Performances On Television Shows, Such As "The Tonight Show Starring Jimmy Fallon," Further Showcased Their Musical Rapport And Contributed To Their Crossover Appeal.

"Mtv Unplugged: Tony Bennett" (1994):

Tony Bennett's Appearance On Mtv's "Unplugged" Series In 1994 Brought His Music To A New Generation Of Viewers. The Show Featured Stripped-Down, Acoustic Versions Of His Classic Songs, Highlighting The Timeless Appeal Of His Music. The Album "Mtv Unplugged: Tony Bennett" Received Critical Acclaim And Introduced Tony To Younger Audiences, Further Broadening His Fan Base.

"Tony Bennett: The Music Never Ends" (2007):
In 2007, Hbo Aired A Documentary Titled "Tony Bennett: The Music Never Ends," Directed By Bruce Ricker. The Documentary Provided An Intimate Look At Tony's Life And Career, Featuring Interviews With Tony Himself, As Well As Insights From Family Members, Friends, And Fellow Artists. It Was A Comprehensive Tribute To His Enduring Legacy In The Music Industry.

"Tony Bennett's Wonderful World: Live In San Francisco" (2002):
Recorded At The Fairmont Hotel In San Francisco, "Tony Bennett's Wonderful World: Live In San Francisco" Showcased Tony's Artistry And His Affection For The City That Inspired One Of His Most Famous Songs, "I Left My Heart In San Francisco." The Performance Captured The Magic Of Tony's Live Shows, As He Delivered Heartfelt Renditions Of Classic Songs In Front Of An Enthusiastic Audience.

Film Appearances:
In Addition To His Numerous Television Appearances, Tony Bennett Has Made Memorable Appearances In Several Films. His Role As Himself In The Film "The Oscar" (1966), Starring Stephen Boyd And Elke Sommer, Showcased His Charm And Personality On The Silver Screen. Over The Years, He Has Also Contributed His Voice And Music To Various Film Soundtracks,

Adding To His Influence In The World Of Cinema.

"Amy" (2015):
Tony Bennett's Appearance In The Critically Acclaimed Documentary "Amy" (2015), Which Chronicles The Life And Career Of The Late Singer Amy Winehouse, Was A Poignant Moment. In The Film, Tony Reflects On The Impact Of Addiction On Artists And The Importance Of Recognizing The Struggle Of Those Battling With Substance Abuse. His Insights Provided A Sobering Perspective On The Challenges Faced By Musicians In The Spotlight.

"Bruce Almighty" (2003):
In The Comedy Film "Bruce Almighty" (2003), Tony Bennett Made A Cameo Appearance Alongside Actor Jim Carrey. The Scene, Set In A Jazz Club, Featured Tony Performing "If I Ruled The World," Adding A

Touch Of Elegance And Charm To The Film's Comedic Storyline.

Role As A Mentor To Young Artists

Tony Bennett Has Embraced The Position Of A Mentor To Emerging Artists Throughout His Illustrious Career, Imparting His Expertise, Experience, And Creative Guidance To Assist The Next Generation Of Musicians. Tony Has Been A Source Of Motivation And Encouragement For Budding Singers, Musicians, And Entertainers With His Friendly And Compassionate Demeanor. His Mentoring Has Had An Influence On People's Lives And Careers Off The Stage As Well, Benefiting Those Who Were Lucky Enough To Have It. The Different Ways That Tony Bennett Has Supported And Encouraged Emerging Talent Will Be Highlighted In This Examination Of His Mentoring Role, Nurturing A Legacy That Goes Beyond His Musical Accomplishments.

Tony Bennett Founded The Frank Sinatra School Of The Arts (Fssa) In Astoria, Queens,

New York City, In 2001 As A Result Of His Commitment To Both Education And The Arts. The School Bears Frank Sinatra's Name, Another Legendary Musician Who Was A Close Friend Of His. A Public High School Called Fssa Offers Young Children A Challenging Arts Education In Areas Including Vocal Music, Instrumental Music, Dance, Theater, And Fine Arts.

The Goal Of The School Is To Provide Ambitious Young Artists A Thorough Education That Develops Their Artistic Abilities While Giving Them A Strong Academic Basis. Tony's Commitment In The School Extends Beyond Its Establishment; He Actively Takes Part In Its Initiatives, Often Visits The Kids, And Inspires The School's Future Artists.

Supporting Music Education: Tony Bennett Has Often Emphasized The Need Of Protecting The Arts In Schools As A

Supporter Of Music Education. He Is Aware Of The Transforming Influence That Arts Education Has In Nurturing Young People's Creativity. Through His Personal Experiences, He Has Come To Understand The Good Effects That Exposure To The Arts Can Have On A Person's Life, Regardless Of The Job Route They Choose.

Tony's Love Of Music Education Has Inspired Him To Sponsor Projects That Bring The Arts And Music To Neglected Areas. He Has Taken Part In Fundraising Efforts And Occasions Meant To Provide Young Artists Access To Top-Notch Arts Education By Offering Them Resources And Opportunity.

Collaborations With Young Musicians: Tony Bennett's Mentoring Style Is Characterized By His Desire To Work With Young And Rising Musicians. He Has Welcomed The Chance To Engage With A New Generation Of Performers Rather Than Seeing Them As

Competitors. His Collaborations Have Produced Engaging Performances That Cross Generational Boundaries And Demonstrate The Everlasting Nature Of Great Music.

Tony's Collaboration With Lady Gaga Is Among The Most Illustrative Instances Of Mentoring At Work. Along With Introducing Gaga To The Great American Songbook, Their 2014 Album "Cheek To Cheek" Duet Also Cemented Their Relationship As Musical Partners. Throughout Their Relationship, Tony's Advice And Encouragement Were Crucial To Gaga's Development As A Jazz Singer.

Tony Bennett's Mentorship Approach Places A Strong Emphasis On The Value Of Authenticity In An Artist's Work. He Advocates For Real Expression Rather Than Giving In To Trends Or Outside Forces, Urging Young Performers To Be Loyal To Themselves And Their Creative Vision.

Young Artists May Learn A Lot From Tony's Own Creative Career, Which Was Characterized By A Commitment To His Profession And A Reluctance To Compromise His Artistic Integrity. He Instills Confidence In His Mentees So They May Successfully Traverse The Hurdles Of The Music Business By Emphasizing The Value Of Discovering One's Own Distinctive Voice And Style.

Career Advice: Throughout His Mentoring, Tony Bennett Kindly Imparts The Knowledge He Has Acquired Over The Course Of His Successful Career. On Voice Technique, Stage Presence, And Engaging An Audience, He Offers Helpful Guidance. Young Musicians May Learn A Lot From His Experiences Performing In A Variety Of Venues, From Small Bars To Large Concert Halls, As They Navigate Their Own Careers.

For Individuals Looking For Advice On Their Creative Adventures, Tony's Tales Of Working With Renowned Artists And Performers, As Well As The Difficulties He Has Encountered And Overcame, Are Of Immeasurable Value. He Places A Strong Emphasis On The Value Of Devotion, Persistence, And The Quest Of Perfection While Perfecting A Trade.

Developing Talent On Talent Programs: Tony Bennett, A Seasoned Performer, Has Acted As A Mentor On Talent Programs, Providing His Knowledge And Advice To Novice Competitors. He Offers Candidates A Rare Chance To Learn From An Accomplished Musician Via His Presence And Mentoring, Motivating Them To Develop As Singers And Performers.

Both Competitors And Fans Have Found Resonance With Tony's Constructive Critique And Words Of Encouragement On

These Programs, Which Has Had A Good Effect On Their Creative Growth.

Personal Connections With Mentees: Tony Bennett Takes A Very Personal Approach To Mentoring, Building Sincere Relationships With His Mentees. He Really Cares About Their Development Both As Performers And As People, Giving Them His Time And Advice Away From The Stage. Numerous Mentees Have Praised His Warmth And Generosity Toward People He Mentors And Mentioned How Much Of An Impact His Mentoring Has On Their Lives And Careers.

Providing An Example: Tony Bennett Serves As A Mentor By Providing An Example Of Professionalism, Humility, And Respect. Aspiring Artists Might Take Inspiration From His Passion To His Work, His Friendliness With Audiences, And His Unrelenting Commitment To Creative Perfection.

Tony's Ongoing Love Of Music And His Unshakable Commitment To Performance Are Proof Of The Value Of A Lifetime Interest In The Arts. His Continued Dedication To His Craft Serves As An Example For Young And Old Artists Alike, As Well As For Those He Guides.

Mentorship As A Lifelong Goal: Tony Bennett's Mentoring Is Not Limited To A Particular Time Or Place. He Has Remained In Touch With His Mentees Throughout His Career, Continuing To Provide Advice And Assistance Years After Their Original Work Together. His Dedication To Supporting The Development Of Emerging Musicians Goes Beyond The Boundaries Of The Music Business, Displaying A Sincere Desire To Have A Long-Lasting Influence On Those He Teaches.

The Legacy Of Mentorship: Tony Bennett's Influence On Those He Has Influenced May

Be Seen In Their Success And Creative Development. Many Of His Mentees Have Gone On To Have Fruitful Careers In Music And The Arts, And They Often Attribute A Large Part Of Their Growth As Artists To Tony.

Beyond His Direct Mentees, Tony Bennett's Mentoring Has A Lasting Impact On The Whole Creative Community. Numerous Musicians Have Been Moved By His Dedication To Encouraging The Next Generation Of Musicians To Embrace Mentoring, Which Has Had A Positive Knock-On Impact In The Music Business.

An Inspirational Source: Tony Bennett's Mentoring Is Defined By Support, Affirmation, And Faith In The Potential Of Young Talent. He Encourages A Culture Of Development And Innovation, Giving His Mentees The Freedom To Take Calculated

Chances And Confidently Follow Their
Creative Goals.

It Serves As A Reminder Of The Influence
That Seasoned Musicians May Have On The
Future Of The Arts Because Tony Is Prepared
To Encourage And Promote Budding Artists.
His Mentoring Is A Perfect Example Of The
Influence A Helping Hand And A Motivating
Presence Can Have On The Professional
Paths Of Aspiring Artists.

Long-Lasting Bonds: Tony Bennett's
Mentoring Often Results In Long-Lasting
Friendships With People He Mentors, In
Addition To The Creative Assistance He
Offers. His Honesty Is Shown In The Sincere
Relationships He Makes With Young Artists,
Which Emphasizes The Individualized
Character Of His Mentoring.

These Strong Ties Underscore The
Reciprocal Nature Of The Connection And

Attest To The Beneficial Effects Of Mentoring On Both The Mentee And The Mentor.

Supporting Diversity: In Addition To Being A Mentor, Tony Bennett Has Supported Diversity In The Arts. He Appreciates The Value Of Many Voices And Viewpoints Being Represented In Music And Entertainment. His Mentoring Is Diversified, Encouraging Young Talent From Many Backgrounds And Promoting An Inclusive And Creative Atmosphere.

Paying It Forward: Tony Bennett's Dedication To Mentoring Endures Despite The Success Of His Successful Career. He Is Still Committed To Advancing The Value Of Arts Education And Helping Emerging Artists. His Continued Mentoring Efforts Serve As A Constant Reminder Of The Immense Influence One Artist Can Have On The Lives And Careers Of Several Others.

In Conclusion, One Of The Distinguishing Characteristics Of Tony Bennett's Remarkable Career Has Been His Position As A Mentor To Emerging Musicians. His Commitment To Developing Talent, Imparting Knowledge, And Encouraging The Next Generation Of Artists Has Irrevocably Changed The Face Of Music And The Arts. Tony Has Mentored Innumerable Budding Artists, Giving Them The Direction And Inspiration They Needed To Follow Their Creative Interests With Assurance And Sincerity. His Deep And Eternal Effect On The Musical World Will Be Preserved Through His Lasting Legacy As A Mentor, Which Will Continue To Alter The Course Of Music.

Performances At Notable Events And Venues

The Fact That Tony Bennett Has Been Invited To Play At Such Prestigious Events And Places Speaks Volumes About His Status As One Of The Most Beloved And Recognizable Figures In American Music. Tony's Live Performances Have Enthralled Audiences All Around The Globe, From His Early Days In Small Bars To His Current Status As A Headliner At Renowned Events And Famous Locations. The Highlights Of His Career As A Beloved Performer And Cultural Ambassador Will Be Highlighted In This Investigation Of His Appearances At Important Events And Places.

Tony Bennett's Concerts In Carnegie Hall Are Among The Most Storied Chapters Of His Illustrious Career. In 1962, He Had A Performance In The Legendary Hall And Later Released A Live Cd Titled "Tony Bennett At Carnegie Hall." The Cd Became

One Of His Most Revered Releases Because
It So Well Captured The Energy And
Excitement Of His Live Performance. Tony's
Following Performances At Carnegie Hall
Further Solidified His Standing As A
Fascinating Live Performer.

Many Presidents Have Asked Tony Bennett
To Sing At The White House, And He Has
Gladly Accepted. He Has Been A Much-
Loved Performer For Many Administrations
After Appearing At Inaugurations, State
Banquets, And Other High-Profile Occasions.
His Invitation To Perform At The White
House Is Evidence Of His Standing As A
Musical And Artistic Ambassador For The
United States.

In 2005, Tony Bennett Was Recognized For
His Musical Contributions To The World By
Receiving The Kennedy Center Honors. At
The Celebration, Tony's Peers Paid Homage
To Him By Singing His Most Famous Songs,

Demonstrating The Widespread Influence Of His Work In The Entertainment Industry. The Kennedy Center Honors Are Considered Among The Most Prestigious Awards In The Arts In The United States.

Tony Bennett Has Made Annual Appearances At The Grammy Awards A Staple Of His Career. Many Times He Has Performed On The Grammy Stage, And Each Time His Strong Voice And Fresh Takes On Old Favorites Have Wowed The Crowd. Tony Has Won A Total Of 20 Grammy Awards, Not Considering The Several Victories He Has Racked Up For Best Traditional Pop Vocal Album Throughout His Time As A Contender.

The 1996 Rendition Of "Fly Me To The Moon" By Tony Bennett On The Super Bowl Xxx Pre-Game Program Was An Unforgettable Moment For Football Fans And Music Aficionados Alike. With The Florida Orchestra Providing

Accompaniment, His Performance Of The Legendary Song Set The Mood For A Magical Super Bowl.

The American Singer Tony Bennett Has Become A Tradition During July 4th Festivities With His Stirring Performances Of Patriotic Standards Like "America The Beautiful." His Annual Attendance At 4th Of July Events Has Become A Tradition That People Look Forward To Every Year.

Tony Bennett Has Built A Name For Himself At The Academy Awards By Contributing To Iconic Moments In Oscar History With His Performances Of Oscar-Nominated Songs. His Performances Raised The Profile Of Music In Cinema By Adding A Touch Of Class And Artistry To The Star-Studded Events.

Tony Bennett Has Served As A Cultural Ambassador By Performing At Many United Nations Celebrations, Where He Has

Emphasized The Power Of Music And The Arts To Promote International Harmony And Cooperation. His Performances At These Global Events Have Shown How Music Can Unite People From All Around The World.

A New Generation Of Music Fans Was Exposed To Tony Bennett In 1994 When He Appeared On Mtv's "Unplugged" Series. In Order To Demonstrate The Universality Of His Music And Its Continued Relevance To Younger Audiences, He Performed Acoustic Renditions Of His Iconic Tunes.

Tony Bennett's New Year's Eve Shows Have Become An Annual Event For Music Lovers Throughout The Globe. His Visits In Numerous Locations, Including New York City's Times Square, Have Helped Usher In The New Year With Celebration And Hope.

Tony Bennett Brought His Characteristic Soft Voice And Charisma To The World-Famous

Tennis Tournament In 2009 As He Sang "The Best Is Yet To Come" At The Wimbledon Championships. The Sophistication He Brought To The Sports Event Was Indicative Of His Broad Popularity.

A Favorite Holiday Ritual In The Nation's Capital Is Listening To Tony Bennett Play During The Annual Lighting Of The National Christmas Tree. His Performances Of Well-Known Christmas Tunes Have Brought Cheer To The Event's Attendees.

Tony Bennett's Performance During The Closing Ceremony Of The 2012 London Olympics Was A Highlight Of The Event's Cultural Importance. The Success Of His Songs Throughout The World Was Highlighted By His Presence.

Tony Bennett Has Been A Regular At The Monterey Jazz Festival, Often Considered To Be The Pinnacle Of Jazz Festivals Worldwide.

His Performances At The Festival Have Solidified His Status As A Jazz Legend And Brought Attention To The Significance Of His Work In The Field.

Tony Bennett's Performances At The Royal Variety Show In The Uk Have Wowed Crowds And Shown His Global Popularity. His Performances For The British Royal Family Are Representative Of His Standing As A Worldwide Performer.

Numerous Concerts And Galas Have Been Held In Tony Bennett's Honor To Recognize His Impact On Music And Culture At Large. Artists From All Around The Entertainment Industry Have Performed At These Events To Celebrate Tony's Life And Career.

New York City's Radio City Music Hall: Tony Bennett's Concerts There Have Attracted Fans From All Over The Globe Thanks To Their Legendary Status. Despite The Passage

Of Time, His Reputation As A Live Performer Remains Strong, As Seen By The Sold-Out Audiences And Standing Ovations For His Appearances At The Historic Arena.

Tony Bennett Has Wowed West Coast Audiences With His Personality And Skill At The Hollywood Bowl In Los Angeles. The Impressions He Made On Audiences At The Historic Amphitheater Helped To Cement His Reputation As A Legendary Performer.

Tony Bennett's Performances At The Ravinia Festival In Highland Park, Illinois, Are Widely Regarded As Some Of The Pianist's Finest Work. His Performances In The Amphitheater Have Become Must-See Events Of The Festival.

Frank Sinatra's Close Friend And Contemporaries, The Legendary Singer's Music Has Been Honored On Multiple Times By Tony Bennett. His Renditions Of Sinatra's

Songs Have Always Been Respectful And
Moving, Befitting The Chairman Of The
Board's Legacy.

Tony Bennett's Concert Tours Have Brought
Him To Locations All Over The Globe, Where
His Ageless Music And Magnetic Stage
Presence Have Wowed Crowds. His Tours
Have Taken Him To Illustrious Venues All
Around The World, Including Theaters,
Music Halls, And Stadiums.

Tony Bennett's Worldwide Influence As A
Cultural Ambassador Has Been Boosted By
His Appearances At Festivals Across The
World. The Fact That He Has Been Invited To
Perform At Festivals All Around The World,
Including In Europe, Asia, And Beyond, Is A
Testament To The Music's Global Popularity.

Tony Bennett's Memorial Performances At
Washington, D.C.'S National Memorial Day
Concert Have Been Very Moving Acts Of

Remembering And Honor In Recent Years.
He Has Performed Patriotic Songs That Pay
Tribute To The Service Of Our Nation's
Heroes.

Tony Bennett Has Donated His Time And
Skill To Many Benefit Performances
Throughout The Course Of His Career, All In
The Name Of Helping Those In Need. Funds
And Awareness For Many Causes Have Been
Increased Because To His Appearances At
These Occasions.

Tony Bennett's Attendance At Charity Galas
And Fundraisers Have Boosted The Events'
Profile And Garnered More Charitable
Contributions For A Wide Range Of
Organizations.

Joint Concerts Between Tony Bennett And
Lady Gaga Have Been A Highlight Of His
Performances In Recent Years. The Musical
Synergy Between The Two Performers Has

Been On Full Display During Their Joint Performances, Which Have Drawn Passionate Crowds.

Special Tribute Concerts: Tony Bennett Has Not Only Had Tribute Concerts Held In His Honor, But He Has Also Performed In Tribute Concerts For Other Music Legends. He Has Shown His Appreciation For His Fellow Artists By His Participation In Various Events.

Tony Bennett's Performances At Presidential Inaugurations Have Solidified His Place In History As A National Treasure. His Participation In These Landmark Events Has Infused The Celebrations With A Spirit Of Patriotism And Solidarity.

Finally, Tony Bennett's Performances At Major Events And Landmark Sites Have Shown His Evergreen Brilliance, Charisma, And Continuing Popularity. Tony's Live

Performances Have Made A Lasting Impression On The World Of Music And Popular Culture, From Little Jazz Clubs To Huge Concert Halls, From The White House To The Kennedy Center, And From The Super Bowl To Worldwide Venues. His Passion To His Profession, His Unyielding Pursuit Of Creative Greatness, And His Ability To Connect With Audiences Of All Ages Have Made Him A Legend In The Entertainment World And A Cherished Cultural Ambassador. Tony Bennett's Appearances At These Landmarks Have Been Immortalized In Song And Serve As Additional Proof Of His Status As A Music Legend.

Death

Although The Official Cause Of Bennett's Death Has Not Been Disclosed, The Alzheimer's Disease That He Had Been Diagnosed With In 2016 Was A Known Contributor. Sir Elton John Was The First To Pay Homage To Tony On Social Media, Stating In A Statement That He Was "So Sad To Hear Of Tony's Passing" And Posting It On His Instagram Account.

Printed in Poland
by Amazon Fulfillment
Poland Sp. z o.o., Wrocław
06 September 2023